I0010676

NISTIR 8228

Considerations for Managing Internet of Things (IoT) Cybersecurity and Privacy Risks

Katie Boeckl
Michael Fagan
William Fisher
Naomi Lefkovitz
Katerina N. Megas
Ellen Nadeau
Danna Gabel O'Rourke
Ben Piccarreta
Karen Scarfone

National Institute of
Standards and Technology
U.S. Department of Commerce

FORWARD/COMMENTARY

The National Institute of Standards and Technology (NIST) is a measurement standards laboratory, and a non-regulatory agency of the **United States Department of Commerce**. Its mission is to promote innovation and industrial competitiveness. Founded in 1901, as the National Bureau of Standards, NIST was formed with the mandate to provide standard weights and measures, and to serve as the national physical laboratory for the United States. With a world-class measurement and testing laboratory encompassing a wide range of areas of computer science, mathematics, statistics, and systems engineering, NIST's cybersecurity program supports its overall mission to promote U.S. innovation and industrial competitiveness by advancing measurement science, standards, and related technology through research and development in ways that enhance economic security and improve our quality of life.

The need for cybersecurity standards and best practices that address interoperability, usability and privacy has been shown to be critical for the nation. NIST's cybersecurity programs seek to enable greater development and application of practical, innovative security technologies and methodologies that enhance the country's ability to address current and future computer and information security challenges.

The cybersecurity publications produced by NIST cover a wide range of cybersecurity concepts that are carefully designed to work together to produce a holistic approach to cybersecurity primarily for government agencies and constitute the best practices used by industry. This holistic strategy to cybersecurity covers the gamut of security subjects from development of secure encryption standards for communication and storage of information while at rest to how best to recover from a cyber-attack.

Why buy a book you can download for free?   We print this so you don't have to.

Some are available only in electronic media. Some online docs are missing pages or barely legible.

We at 4th Watch Publishing are former government employees, so we know how government employees actually use the standards. When a new standard is released, an engineer prints it out, punches holes and puts it in a 3-ring binder. While this is not a big deal for a 5 or 10-page document, many NIST documents are over 100 pages and printing a large document is a time-consuming effort. So, an engineer that's paid $75 an hour is spending hours simply printing out the tools needed to do the job. That's time that could be better spent doing engineering. We publish these documents so engineers can focus on what they were hired to do – engineering. It's much more cost-effective to just order the latest version from Amazon.com

If there is a standard you would like published, let us know. Our web site is usgovpub.com

Many of our titles are available as eBooks for Kindle, iPad, Nook, remarkable, BOOX, and Sony eReaders. Buy the paperback from Amazon and get Kindle eBook FREE using MATCHBOOK. Go to https://usgovpub.com to learn more.

Why buy an eBook when you can access data on a website for free? HYPERLINKS

Yes, many books are available as a PDF, but not all PDFs are bookmarked? Do you really want to search a 6,500-page PDF document manually? Load our copy onto your Kindle, PC, iPad, Android Tablet, Nook, or iPhone (download the FREE kindle App from the APP Store) and you have an easily searchable copy. Most devices will allow you to easily navigate an ePub to any Chapter. Note that there is a distinction between a Table of Contents and "Page Navigation". Page Navigation refers to a different sort of Table of Contents. Not one appearing as a page in the book, but one that shows up on the device itself when the reader accesses the navigation feature. Readers can click on a navigation link to jump to a Chapter or Subchapter. Once there, most devices allow you to "pinch and zoom" in or out to easily read the text. (Unfortunately, downloading the free sample file at Amazon.com does not include this feature. You have to buy a copy to get that functionality, but as inexpensive as eBooks are, it's worth it.) Kindle allows you to do word search and Page Flip (temporary place holder takes you back when you want to go back and check something). Visit **USGOVPUB.COM** to learn more.

NISTIR 8228

Considerations for Managing Internet of Things (IoT) Cybersecurity and Privacy Risks

Katie Boeckl
Michael Fagan
William Fisher
Naomi Lefkovitz
Katerina N. Megas
Ellen Nadeau
Ben Piccarreta*
Applied Cybersecurity Division
Information Technology Laboratory

Danna Gabel O'Rourke
Deloitte & Touche LLP
Arlington, Virginia

Karen Scarfone
Scarfone Cybersecurity
Clifton, Virginia

*Former employee; all work for this
publication was done while at NIST

June 2019

U.S. Department of Commerce
Wilbur L. Ross, Jr., Secretary

National Institute of Standards and Technology
Walter Copan, NIST Director and Under Secretary of Commerce for Standards and Technology

National Institute of Standards and Technology Interagency or Internal Report 8228
44 pages (June 2019)

This publication is available free of charge from:
https://doi.org/10.6028/NIST.IR.8228

Comments on this publication may be submitted to:

National Institute of Standards and Technology
Attn: Applied Cybersecurity Division, Information Technology Laboratory
100 Bureau Drive (Mail Stop 2000) Gaithersburg, MD 20899-2000
Email: iotsecurity@nist.gov

All comments are subject to release under the Freedom of Information Act (FOIA).

Reports on Computer Systems Technology

The Information Technology Laboratory (ITL) at the National Institute of Standards and Technology (NIST) promotes the U.S. economy and public welfare by providing technical leadership for the Nation's measurement and standards infrastructure. ITL develops tests, test methods, reference data, proof of concept implementations, and technical analyses to advance the development and productive use of information technology. ITL's responsibilities include the development of management, administrative, technical, and physical standards and guidelines for the cost-effective security and privacy of other than national security-related information in federal information systems.

Abstract

The Internet of Things (IoT) is a rapidly evolving and expanding collection of diverse technologies that interact with the physical world. Many organizations are not necessarily aware of the large number of IoT devices they are already using and how IoT devices may affect cybersecurity and privacy risks differently than conventional information technology (IT) devices do. The purpose of this publication is to help federal agencies and other organizations better understand and manage the cybersecurity and privacy risks associated with their individual IoT devices throughout the devices' lifecycles. This publication is the introductory document providing the foundation for a planned series of publications on more specific aspects of this topic.

Keywords

cybersecurity risk; Internet of Things (IoT); privacy risk; risk management; risk mitigation.

Acknowledgments

The authors wish to thank all contributors to this publication, including the participants in the workshops and other interactive sessions, the individuals and organizations from the public and private sectors who provided comments on the preliminary ideas, and the following individuals from NIST: Curt Barker, Matt Barrett, Barbara Cuthill, Donna Dodson, Jim Foti, Ned Goren, Nelson Hastings, Jody Jacobs, Suzanne Lightman, Jeff Marron, Vicky Pillitteri, Tim Polk, Matt Scholl, Eric Simmon, Matt Smith, Murugiah Souppaya, Jim St. Pierre, Kevin Stine, and David Wollman.

Audience

The primary audience for this publication is personnel at federal agencies with responsibilities related to managing cybersecurity and privacy risks for IoT devices, although personnel at other organizations may also find value in the content. Personnel within the following Workforce Categories and Specialty Areas from the National Initiative for Cybersecurity Education (NICE) Cybersecurity Workforce Framework [1] are most likely to find this publication of interest, as are their privacy counterparts:

- Securely Provision (SP): Risk Management (RSK), Systems Architecture (ARC), Systems Development (SYS)
- Operate and Maintain (OM): Data Administration (DTA), Network Services (NET), Systems Administration (ADM), Systems Analysis (ANA)
- Oversee and Govern (OV): Cybersecurity Management (MGT), Executive Cyber Leadership (EXL), Program/Project Management (PMA) and Acquisition
- Protect and Defend (PR): Cybersecurity Defense Analysis (CDA), Cybersecurity Defense Infrastructure Support (INF), Incident Response (CIR), Vulnerability Assessment and Management (VAM)
- Investigate (IN): Digital Forensics (FOR)

In addition, IoT device manufacturers and integrators may find this publication useful for understanding concerns regarding managing cybersecurity and privacy risks for IoT devices.

Note to Readers

Appendix A previously held examples of possible cybersecurity and privacy capabilities that organizations may want their IoT devices to have. That content has been removed from this publication and will be refined and released in a separate publication.

Trademark Information

All registered trademarks and trademarks belong to their respective organizations.

Executive Summary

The Internet of Things (IoT) is a rapidly evolving and expanding collection of diverse technologies that interact with the physical world. IoT devices are an outcome of combining the worlds of information technology (IT) and operational technology (OT). Many IoT devices are the result of the convergence of cloud computing, mobile computing, embedded systems, big data, low-price hardware, and other technological advances. IoT devices can provide computing functionality, data storage, and network connectivity for equipment that previously lacked them, enabling new efficiencies and technological capabilities for the equipment, such as remote access for monitoring, configuration, and troubleshooting. IoT can also add the abilities to analyze data about the physical world and use the results to better inform decision making, alter the physical environment, and anticipate future events.

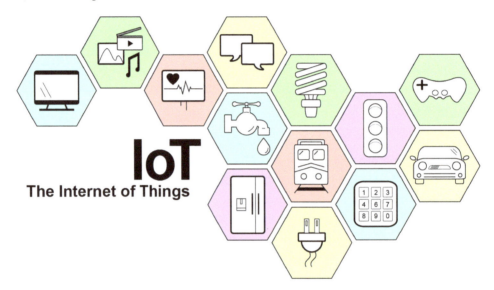

While the full scope of IoT is not precisely defined, it is clearly vast. Every sector has its own types of IoT devices, such as specialized hospital equipment in the healthcare sector and smart road technologies in the transportation sector, and there is a large number of enterprise IoT devices that every sector can use. Versions of nearly every consumer electronics device, many of which are also present in organizations' facilities, have become connected IoT devices—kitchen appliances, thermostats, home security cameras, door locks, light bulbs, and TVs. [2]

Many organizations are not necessarily aware they are using a large number of IoT devices. It is important that organizations understand their use of IoT because many IoT devices affect cybersecurity and privacy risks differently than conventional IT devices do. Once organizations are aware of their existing IoT usage and possible future usage, they need to understand how the characteristics of IoT affect managing cybersecurity and privacy risks, especially in terms of risk response—accepting, avoiding, mitigating, sharing, or transferring risk.

This publication identifies three high-level considerations that may affect the management of cybersecurity and privacy risks for IoT devices as compared to conventional IT devices:

1. **Many IoT devices interact with the physical world in ways conventional IT devices usually do not.** The potential impact of some IoT devices making changes to physical

systems and thus affecting the physical world needs to be explicitly recognized and addressed from cybersecurity and privacy perspectives. Also, operational requirements for performance, reliability, resilience, and safety may be at odds with common cybersecurity and privacy practices for conventional IT devices.

2. **Many IoT devices cannot be accessed, managed, or monitored in the same ways conventional IT devices can.** This can necessitate doing tasks manually for large numbers of IoT devices, expanding staff knowledge and tools to include a much wider variety of IoT device software, and addressing risks with manufacturers and other third parties having remote access or control over IoT devices.

3. **The availability, efficiency, and effectiveness of cybersecurity and privacy capabilities are often different for IoT devices than conventional IT devices.** This means organizations may have to select, implement, and manage additional controls, as well as determine how to respond to risk when sufficient controls for mitigating risk are not available.

Cybersecurity and privacy risks for IoT devices can be thought of in terms of three high-level risk mitigation goals:

1. **Protect device security**. In other words, prevent a device from being used to conduct attacks, including participating in distributed denial of service (DDoS) attacks against other organizations, and eavesdropping on network traffic or compromising other devices on the same network segment. This goal applies to all IoT devices.

2. **Protect data security.** Protect the confidentiality, integrity, and/or availability of data (including personally identifiable information [PII]) collected by, stored on, processed by, or transmitted to or from the IoT device. This goal applies to each IoT device except those without any data that needs protection.

3. **Protect individuals' privacy.** Protect individuals' privacy impacted by PII processing beyond risks managed through device and data security protection. This goal applies to all IoT devices that process PII or that directly or indirectly impact individuals.

Each goal builds on the previous goal and does not replace it or negate the need for it. Meeting each of the risk mitigation goals involves addressing a set of risk mitigation areas. Each risk mitigation area defines an aspect of cybersecurity or privacy risk mitigation thought to be most significantly or unexpectedly affected for IoT by the risk considerations. For each risk mitigation area, there are one or more expectations organizations usually have for how conventional IT devices help mitigate cybersecurity and privacy risks for the area. Finally, there are one or more challenges that IoT devices may pose to each expectation. The figure below depicts the end result of these linkages, which is the identification of a structured set of potential challenges with mitigating cybersecurity and privacy risk for IoT devices that can each be traced back to the relevant risk considerations.

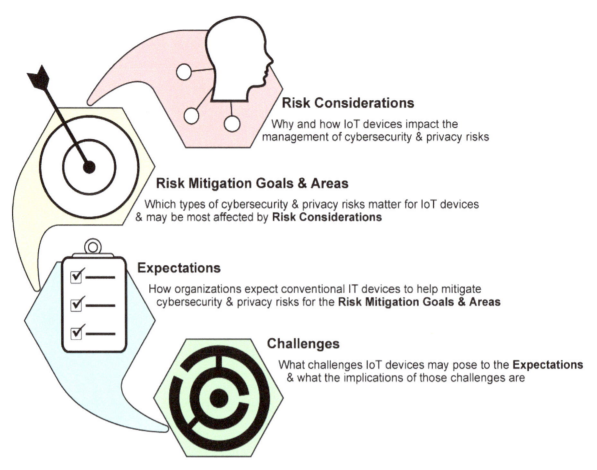

Risk Considerations

Why and how IoT devices impact the management of cybersecurity & privacy risks

Risk Mitigation Goals & Areas

Which types of cybersecurity & privacy risks matter for IoT devices & may be most affected by **Risk Considerations**

Expectations

How organizations expect conventional IT devices to help mitigate cybersecurity & privacy risks for the **Risk Mitigation Goals & Areas**

Challenges

What challenges IoT devices may pose to the **Expectations** & what the implications of those challenges are

Organizations should ensure they are addressing the cybersecurity and privacy risk considerations and challenges throughout the IoT device lifecycle for the appropriate risk mitigation goals and areas. This publication provides the following recommendations for accomplishing this:

1. Understand the IoT device risk considerations and the challenges they may cause to mitigating cybersecurity and privacy risks for IoT devices in the appropriate risk mitigation areas.

2. Adjust organizational policies and processes to address the cybersecurity and privacy risk mitigation challenges throughout the IoT device lifecycle. This publication cites many examples of possible challenges, but each organization will need to customize these to take into account its mission requirements and other organization-specific characteristics.

3. Implement updated mitigation practices for the organization's IoT devices as you would any other changes to practices.

Table of Contents

List of Appendices

List of Figures

List of Tables

1 Introduction

1.1 Purpose and Scope

The purpose of this publication is to help organizations better understand and manage the cybersecurity and privacy risks associated with individual Internet of Things (IoT) devices throughout the devices' lifecycles. This publication emphasizes what makes managing these risks different for IoT devices in general, including consumer, enterprise, and industrial IoT devices, than conventional information technology (IT) devices. It omits all aspects of risk management that are largely the same for IoT and conventional IT, including all aspects of risk management beyond the IoT devices themselves, because these are already addressed by many other risk management publications.

The publication provides insights to inform organizations' risk management processes. After reading this publication, an organization should be able to improve the quality of its risk assessments for IoT devices and its response to the identified risk through the lens of cybersecurity and privacy. However, this does not mean cybersecurity and privacy risks for an IoT device can all be addressed within the device itself. Every IoT device operates within a broader IoT environment where it interacts with other IoT and non-IoT devices, cloud-based services, people, and other components.

For some IoT devices, additional types of risks, including safety, reliability, and resiliency, need to be managed simultaneously with cybersecurity and privacy risks because of the effects addressing one type of risk can have on others. Only cybersecurity and privacy risks are in scope for this publication. Readers who are particularly interested in better understanding other types of risks and their relationship to cybersecurity and privacy may benefit from reading NIST Special Publication (SP) 800-82 Revision 2, *Guide to Industrial Control Systems (ICS) Security*, which provides an operational technology (OT) perspective on cybersecurity and privacy. [3]

Readers do not need a technical understanding of IoT device composition and capabilities, but a basic understanding of cybersecurity and privacy principles is expected.

1.2 Publication Structure

The remainder of this publication is organized into the following major sections and appendices:

- Section 2 defines capabilities IoT devices can provide that are of primary interest in terms of potentially affecting cybersecurity and privacy risk.

- Section 3 describes considerations that may affect the management of cybersecurity and privacy risks for IoT devices.

- Section 4 explores how the risk considerations may affect mitigating cybersecurity and privacy risk for IoT devices. The section lists expectations for how these risks are mitigated in conventional IT environments, then explains how IoT presents challenges to those expectations and what the potential implications of those challenges are.

- Section 5 provides recommendations for organizations on how to address the cybersecurity and privacy risk mitigation challenges for their IoT devices.

- Appendix A previously held examples of possible cybersecurity and privacy capabilities that organizations may want their IoT devices to have. That content has been removed from this publication and will be refined and released in a separate publication.

- Appendix B provides an acronym and abbreviation list.

- Appendix C contains a glossary of selected terms used in the publication.

- Appendix D lists the references for the publication.

Figure 1 depicts the topics covered in each section and subsection of this publication.

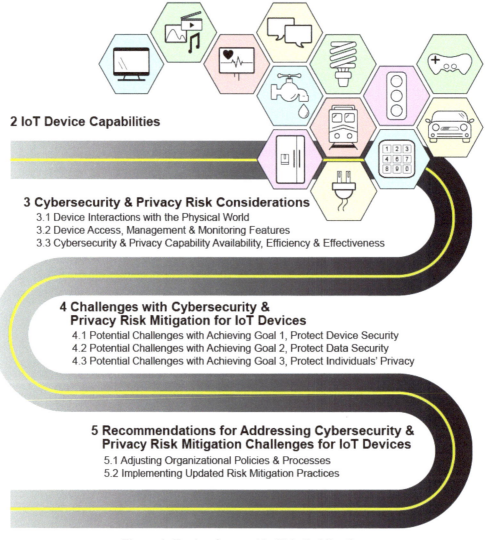

Figure 1: Topics Covered in This Publication

2   IoT Device Capabilities

Each IoT device provides *capabilities*—features or functions—it can use on its own or in conjunction with other IoT and non-IoT devices to achieve one or more goals. This publication references the following types of capabilities IoT devices can provide that are of primary interest in terms of potentially affecting cybersecurity and privacy risk differently than conventional IT devices. This is not a comprehensive list of all possible IoT device capabilities.

- *Transducer capabilities* interact with the physical world and serve as the edge between digital and physical environments. Transducer capabilities provide the ability for computing devices to interact directly with physical entities of interest. Every IoT device has at least one transducer capability. The two types of transducer capabilities are:

    o *Sensing*: the ability to provide an observation of an aspect of the physical world in the form of measurement data. Examples include temperature measurement, radiographic imaging, optical sensing, and audio sensing.

    o *Actuating*: the ability to change something in the physical world. Examples of actuating capabilities include heating coils, cardiac electric shock delivery, electronic door locks, unmanned aerial vehicle operation, servo motors, and robotic arms.

- *Interface capabilities* enable device interactions (e.g., device-to-device communications, human-to-device communications). The types of interface capabilities are:

    o *Application interface*: the ability for other computing devices to communicate with an IoT device through an IoT device application. An example of an application interface capability is an application programming interface (API).

    o *Human user interface*: the ability for an IoT device and people to communicate directly with each other. Examples of human user interface capabilities include touch screens, haptic devices, microphones, cameras, and speakers.

    o *Network interface*: the ability to interface with a communication network for the purpose of communicating data to or from an IoT device—in other words, to use a communication network. A network interface capability includes both hardware and software (e.g., a network interface card or chip and the software implementation of the networking protocol that uses the card or chip). Examples of network interface capabilities include Ethernet, Wi-Fi, Bluetooth, Long-Term Evolution (LTE), and ZigBee. Every IoT device has at least one enabled network interface capability and may have more than one.

- *Supporting capabilities* provide functionality that supports the other IoT capabilities. Examples are device management, cybersecurity, and privacy capabilities. [2]

Figure 2 summarizes these IoT device capabilities.

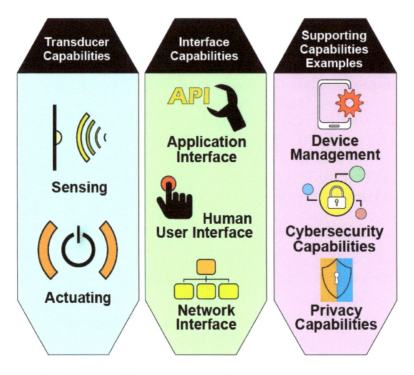

Figure 2: IoT Device Capabilities Potentially Affecting Cybersecurity and Privacy Risk

3   Cybersecurity and Privacy Risk Considerations

Cybersecurity risk and privacy risk are related but distinct concepts. *Risk* is defined in NIST SP 800-37 Revision 2 as "a measure of the extent to which an entity is threatened by a potential circumstance or event, and typically is a function of: (i) the adverse impact, or magnitude of harm, that would arise if the circumstance or event occurs; and (ii) the likelihood of occurrence." [4] For cybersecurity, risk is about threats—the exploitation of vulnerabilities by threat actors to compromise device or data confidentiality, integrity, or availability. For privacy, risk is about *problematic data actions*—operations that process personally identifiable information (PII) through the information lifecycle to meet mission or business needs of an organization or "authorized" PII processing and, as a side effect, cause individuals to experience some type of problem(s). As Figure 3 depicts, privacy and cybersecurity risk overlap with respect to concerns about the cybersecurity of PII, but there are also privacy concerns without implications for cybersecurity, and cybersecurity concerns without implications for privacy. [5]

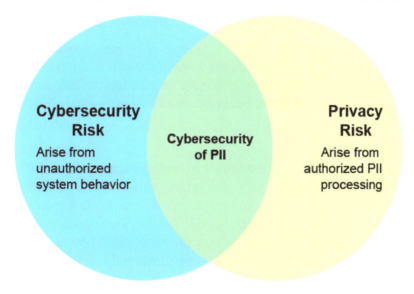

Figure 3: Relationship Between Cybersecurity and Privacy Risks

IoT devices generally face the same types of cybersecurity and privacy risks as conventional IT devices, though the prevalence and severity of such risks often differ. For example, data security risks are almost always a significant concern for conventional IT devices, but for some IoT devices, there may not be data security risks because they do not have any data that needs protection.

This section defines three cybersecurity and privacy risk considerations that may affect the management of cybersecurity and privacy risks for IoT devices. Organizations should ensure they are addressing these risk considerations throughout the lifecycle of their IoT devices. Section 4 provides more information on how these risk considerations may affect risk mitigation, and Section 5 provides recommendations for organizations on how to address the risk mitigation challenges.

3.1   Consideration 1: Device Interactions with the Physical World

Many IoT devices interact with the physical world in ways conventional IT devices usually do not.

The interactions with the physical world that IoT devices enable may affect cybersecurity and privacy risks in several ways. Here are examples:

- IoT sensor data, representing measurements of the physical world, always has uncertainties associated with it. Effective management of IoT sensor data, including understanding uncertainties, is necessary to assess data quality and meaning so the organization can make decisions regarding the data's use and avoid introducing new risks. Without this, error rates may be unknown for the different contexts in which an IoT device might be used.[1] Effective IoT sensor data management is important when mitigating physical attacks on sensor technology, such as attacks performed through wireless signals, that could cause sensors to produce false results.

- The ubiquity of IoT sensors in public and private environments can contribute to the aggregation and analysis of enormous amounts of data about individuals. These activities can be used to influence individuals' behavior or decision-making in ways they do not understand, or lead to information being revealed that individuals did not want revealed, including the re-identification of previously de-identified PII—and may be beyond the originally intended scope of the IoT device's operation.

- IoT devices with actuators have the ability to make changes to physical systems and thus affect the physical world. The potential impact of this needs to be explicitly recognized and addressed from cybersecurity and privacy perspectives. In a worst-case scenario, a compromise could allow an attacker to use an IoT device to endanger human safety, damage or destroy equipment and facilities, or cause major operational disruptions. Privacy concerns and related civil liberties concerns could arise through authorized changes to physical systems that could impact individuals' physical autonomy or behavior in personal and public spaces. For example, physical access controls, such as automated door locks, could be used to limit access to rooms or buildings with individuals inside, or environmental controls such as lighting or temperature could be used to influence individuals' movement in buildings.

- IoT network interfaces often enable remote access to physical systems that previously could only be accessed locally. Manufacturers, vendors, and other third parties may be able to use remote access to IoT devices for management, monitoring, maintenance, and troubleshooting purposes. This may put the physical systems accessible through the IoT devices at much greater risk of compromise. Further, these decentralized data processing functions can exacerbate some privacy risks, making it harder for individuals to understand how the IoT system is operating so that they can make informed decisions regarding the processing of their information and their interactions with the IoT system.

---

[1] For more information on measurement uncertainty, see https://www.nist.gov/itl/sed/topic-areas/measurement-uncertainty.

Another important aspect of IoT device interactions with the physical world is the operational requirements devices must meet in various environments and use cases. Many IoT devices must comply with stringent requirements for performance, reliability, resilience, safety, and other objectives. These requirements may be at odds with common cybersecurity and privacy practices for conventional IT. For example, practices such as automatic patching are generally considered essential for conventional IT, but these practices could have far greater negative impacts on some IoT devices with actuators, making critical services unavailable and endangering human safety. An organization might reasonably decide that patches should be installed at a date and time chosen by the organization with the appropriate staff onsite and ready to react immediately if a problem occurs. An organization might also reasonably decide to avoid patching certain IoT devices under normal circumstances and instead tightly restrict logical and physical access to them to prevent exploitation of unpatched vulnerabilities.

Another way to think of this is in terms of general cybersecurity objectives: confidentiality, integrity, and availability. For conventional IT devices, confidentiality often receives the most attention because of the value of data and the consequences of a breach of confidentiality. For many IoT devices, availability and integrity are more important than confidentiality because of the potential impact to the physical world. Imagine an IoT device that is critical for preventing damage to a facility. An attacker who can view the IoT device's stored or transmitted data might not gain any advantage or value from it, but an attacker who can alter the data might trigger a series of events that cause an incident.

3.2   Consideration 2: Device Access, Management, and Monitoring Features

Many IoT devices cannot be accessed, managed, or monitored in the same ways conventional IT devices can.

Conventional IT devices usually provide authorized people, processes, and devices with hardware and software access, management, and monitoring features. In other words, an authorized administrator, process, or device can directly access a conventional IT device's firmware, operating system, and applications, fully manage the device and its software throughout the device's lifecycle as needed, and monitor the internal characteristics and state of the device at all times. Authorized users can also access a restricted subset of the access, management, and monitoring features.

In contrast, many IoT devices are opaque, often referred to as "black boxes." They provide little or no visibility into their state and composition, including the identity of any external services and systems they interact with, and little or no access to and management of their software and configuration. The organization may not know what capabilities an IoT device can provide or is currently providing. In extreme cases, it may be difficult to determine if a black box product is actually an IoT device because of the lack of transparency.

Authorized people, processes, and devices may encounter one or more of the following challenges in accessing, managing, and monitoring IoT devices that affect cybersecurity and privacy risk:

- **Lack of management features.** Administrators may not be able to fully manage an IoT device's firmware, operating system, and applications throughout the IoT device's lifecycle. Unavailable features may include the ability to acquire, verify the integrity of, install, configure, store, retrieve, execute, terminate, remove, replace, update, and patch software. In addition, an IoT device's software may be automatically reconfigured when an adverse event occurs, such as a power failure or a loss of network connectivity.

- **Lack of interfaces.** Some IoT devices lack application and/or human user interfaces for device use and management. When such interfaces do exist, they may not provide the functionality usually offered by conventional IT devices. An example is the challenge in notifying users about an IoT device's processing of their PII so they can provide meaningful consent to this processing. An additional issue is the lack of universally accepted standards for IoT application interfaces, including expressing and formatting data, issuing commands, and otherwise fostering interoperability between IoT devices.

- **Difficulties with management at scale.** Most IoT devices do not support standardized mechanisms for centralized management, and the sheer number of IoT devices to be managed may be overwhelming.

- **Wide variety of software to manage.** There is extensive variety in the software used by IoT devices, including firmware, standard and real-time operating systems, and applications. This significantly complicates software management throughout the IoT device lifecycle, affecting such areas as configuration and patch management.

- **Differing lifespan expectations.** A manufacturer may intend for a particular IoT device to only be used for a few years and then discarded. An organization purchasing that device might want to use it for a longer time, but the manufacturer may stop supporting the device (e.g., releasing patches for known vulnerabilities) either by choice or because of supply chain limitations (e.g., supplier no longer releases patches for a particular IoT device component). The problem of differing lifespan expectations is not new and is not specific to IoT, but it may be particularly important for some IoT devices because of safety, reliability, and other risks potentially involved in using devices past their intended lifespan.

- **Unserviceable hardware.** IoT device hardware may not be serviceable, meaning it cannot be repaired, customized, or inspected internally.

- **Lack of inventory capabilities.** IoT devices brought into an organization may not be inventoried, registered, and otherwise provisioned via the normal IT processes. This is especially true for types of devices that did not previously have networking capabilities.

- **Heterogeneous ownership.** There is often heterogeneous ownership of IoT devices. For example, an IoT device may transfer data to manufacturer-provided cloud-based service processing and storage. Data may also be sent to a cloud service to aggregate data from multiple IoT devices in a single location. These cloud services may have access to portions or all of the devices' data, or even access to and control of the devices themselves for monitoring, maintenance, and troubleshooting purposes. In some cases, only manufacturers have the authority to do maintenance; an organization attempting to install patches or do other maintenance tasks on an IoT device may void the warranty. Also, in IoT there may be little or no information available about device ownership, especially in black box IoT devices. This could exacerbate existing privacy redress difficulties because the lack of accountability limits individuals' abilities to locate the source of and correct or delete information about themselves, or to address other problems. Another concern with heterogeneous ownership is the effect on device reprovisioning—what data may still be available after transferring control of a device.

3.3 Consideration 3: Cybersecurity and Privacy Capability Availability, Efficiency, and Effectiveness

The availability, efficiency, and effectiveness of cybersecurity and privacy capabilities are often different for IoT devices than conventional IT devices.

For the purposes of this publication, built-in cybersecurity and privacy capabilities are called *pre-market capabilities*. Pre-market capabilities are integrated into IoT devices by the manufacturer or vendor before they are shipped to customer organizations. *Post-market capabilities* are those capabilities that organizations select, acquire, and deploy themselves in addition to pre-market capabilities. Pre-market and post-market cybersecurity and privacy capabilities are often different for IoT devices than conventional IT. The main reasons for this are:

- Many IoT devices do not or cannot support the range of cybersecurity and privacy capabilities typically built into conventional IT devices. For example, a "black box" IoT device may not log its cybersecurity and privacy events or may not give organizations access to its logs. If pre-market capabilities are available for IoT devices, they may be inadequate in terms of strength or performance—e.g., using strong encryption and mutual authentication to protect communications may cause unacceptable delays.[2] Post-market capabilities cannot be installed onto many IoT devices. Also, existing pre-market and post-market capabilities may not be able to scale to meet the needs of IoT—for example, an existing network-based cybersecurity appliance for conventional IT devices may not be able to also process the volume of network traffic and generated data from a large number of IoT devices.

- The level of effort needed to manage, monitor, and maintain pre-market capabilities on each IoT device may be excessive. Especially when IoT devices do not support centralized management, it may be more efficient to implement and use centralized post-market capabilities that help protect numerous IoT devices instead of trying to achieve the equivalent level of protection on each individual IoT device. One example is having a single network-based IoT gateway or IoT security gateway protecting many IoT devices instead of having to design, manage, and maintain a unique set of protection capabilities within each IoT device.

- Some post-market capabilities for conventional IT, such as network-based intrusion prevention systems, antimalware servers, and firewalls, may not be as effective at

---

[2] For more information on low-resource computing devices, see Bormann C, Ersue M, Keranen A (2014) Terminology for Constrained-Node Networks. (Internet Engineering Task Force (IETF)), Request for Comments (RFC) 7228. https://doi.org/10.17487/RFC7228.

protecting IoT devices as they are at protecting conventional IT. IoT devices often use protocols that cybersecurity and privacy controls for conventional IT cannot understand and analyze. Also, IoT devices may communicate directly with each other, such as through point-to-point wireless communication, instead of using a monitored infrastructure network.

An IoT device may not need some of the cybersecurity and privacy capabilities conventional IT devices rely on—an example is an IoT device without data storage capabilities not needing to protect data at rest. An IoT device may also need additional capabilities that most conventional IT devices do not use, especially if the IoT device enables new interactions with the physical world.

4   Challenges with Cybersecurity and Privacy Risk Mitigation for IoT Devices

Cybersecurity and privacy risks for IoT devices can be thought of in terms of three high-level *risk mitigation goals*, as shown in Figure 4:

1. **Protect device security**. In other words, prevent a device from being used to conduct attacks, including participating in distributed denial of service (DDoS) attacks against other organizations, and eavesdropping on network traffic or compromising other devices on the same network segment. This goal applies to all IoT devices.

2. **Protect data security.** Protect the confidentiality, integrity, and/or availability of data (including PII) collected by, stored on, processed by, or transmitted to or from the IoT device. This goal applies to each IoT device except those without any data that needs protection.

3. **Protect individuals' privacy.** Protect individuals' privacy impacted by PII processing beyond risks managed through device and data security protection. This goal applies to all IoT devices that process PII or that directly or indirectly impact individuals.

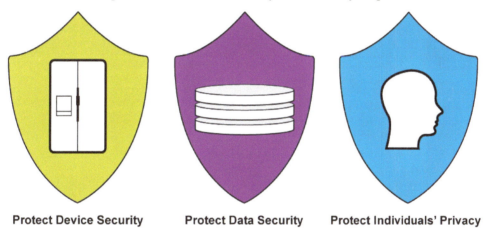

Protect Device Security   Protect Data Security   Protect Individuals' Privacy

Figure 4: Risk Mitigation Goals

Each goal builds on the previous goal and does not replace it or negate the need for it. Meeting each of the risk mitigation goals involves addressing a set of *risk mitigation areas*, which are defined below. Each risk mitigation area defines an aspect of cybersecurity or privacy risk mitigation thought to be most significantly or unexpectedly affected for IoT by the risk considerations defined in Section 3.

Risk mitigation areas for Goal 1, Protect Device Security:

*   **Asset Management:** Maintain a current, accurate inventory of all IoT devices and their relevant characteristics throughout the devices' lifecycles in order to use that information for cybersecurity and privacy risk management purposes.

*   **Vulnerability Management:** Identify and eliminate known vulnerabilities in IoT device software and firmware in order to reduce the likelihood and ease of exploitation and compromise.

- **Access Management:** Prevent unauthorized and improper physical and logical access to, usage of, and administration of IoT devices by people, processes, and other computing devices.

- **Device Security Incident Detection:** Monitor and analyze IoT device activity for signs of incidents involving device security.

Risk mitigation areas for Goal 2, Protect Data Security:

- **Data Protection:** Prevent access to and tampering with data at rest or in transit that might expose sensitive information or allow manipulation or disruption of IoT device operations.

- **Data Security Incident Detection:** Monitor and analyze IoT device activity for signs of incidents involving data security.

Risk mitigation areas for Goal 3, Protect Individuals' Privacy:

- **Information Flow Management:** Maintain a current, accurate mapping of the information lifecycle of PII, including the type of data action, the elements of PII being processed by the data action, the party doing the processing, and any additional relevant contextual factors about the processing to use for privacy risk management purposes.

- **PII Processing Permissions Management:** Maintain permissions for PII processing to prevent unpermitted PII processing.

- **Informed Decision Making:** Enable individuals to understand the effects of PII processing and interactions with the device, participate in decision-making about the PII processing or interactions, and resolve problems.

- **Disassociated Data Management:** Identify authorized PII processing and determine how PII may be minimized or disassociated from individuals and IoT devices.

- **Privacy Breach Detection:** Monitor and analyze IoT device activity for signs of breaches involving individuals' privacy.

Sections 4.1, 4.2, and 4.3 examine how the risk considerations introduce challenges for cybersecurity and privacy risk managers with meeting each of the three risk mitigation goals for an organization's IoT devices—in other words, how mitigation may differ for IoT versus conventional IT. Section 5 provides recommendations on how organizations should address these challenges.

4.1 Potential Challenges with Achieving Goal 1, Protect Device Security

Figure 5 shows the relationships among the Section 3 and Section 4 concepts. Section 3 defines the three risk considerations, which explain why and how IoT devices impact the management of cybersecurity and privacy risks. Next, the Section 4 introduction defines the risk mitigation goals and areas, which specify which types of cybersecurity and privacy risks matter for IoT devices and may be most affected by the risk considerations. The rest of Section 4 lists expectations, which are how organizations expect conventional IT devices to help mitigate cybersecurity and privacy risks for the risk mitigation goals and areas, and the challenges IoT devices may pose to those expectations, along with the implications of those challenges. The end result of these linkages is the identification of a structured set of potential challenges for mitigating cybersecurity and privacy risk for IoT devices that can each be traced back to the relevant risk considerations.

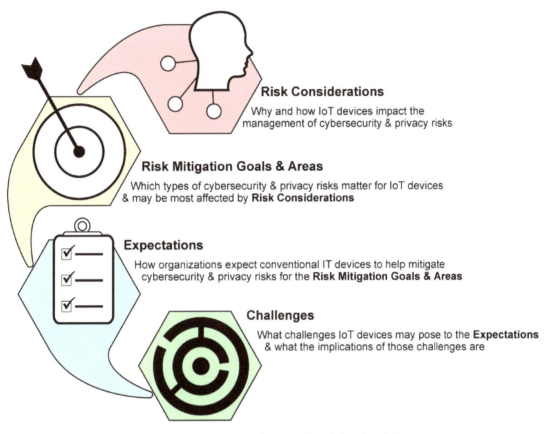

Risk Considerations
Why and how IoT devices impact the management of cybersecurity & privacy risks

Risk Mitigation Goals & Areas
Which types of cybersecurity & privacy risks matter for IoT devices & may be most affected by **Risk Considerations**

Expectations
How organizations expect conventional IT devices to help mitigate cybersecurity & privacy risks for the **Risk Mitigation Goals & Areas**

Challenges
What challenges IoT devices may pose to the **Expectations** & what the implications of those challenges are

Figure 5: Relationships Among Section 3 and Section 4 Concepts

Many readers may not need to use the information at all the levels of detail depicted in Figure 5, and some readers may only need the information at one level, such as the list of challenges. This document includes all the levels in order to explain the basis for identifying these particular challenges as being potentially significant for IoT devices. Also, some readers may be able to use all levels to inform their risk management efforts.

Table 1 lists common expectations for the pre-market capabilities of conventional IT devices that are often used to help mitigate their device security risk. Although these expectations are not always true for conventional IT devices, they are usually true and have greatly influenced common device security practices for conventional IT devices. For each expectation, Table 1 defines one or more potential challenges individual IoT devices may pose to the expectation. Each challenge has its own row in the table:

- First column: a brief statement of the challenge, with each challenge uniquely numbered to make it easy to reference, and the numbers of the risk considerations from Section 3 that cause the challenge.

- Second column: examples of draft NIST SP 800-53 Revision 5 [7] controls that might be negatively affected to some extent for some individual IoT devices.

- Third column: the potential implications for the organization if a substantial number of IoT devices are affected by the challenge.

- Fourth column: examples of Cybersecurity Framework Subcategories [6] that might be negatively affected to some extent by the implications.

The tables in this section do not define or imply equivalence between the NIST SP 800-53 controls and the Cybersecurity Framework Subcategories in each row. For example, in many cases, a challenge affects one aspect of the SP 800-53 controls and a different aspect of the Cybersecurity Framework Subcategories. Additionally, IoT devices not meeting traditional expectations could be a positive for risk mitigation since these limitations could pose *less* risk than when the more robust capability or function is present as per expectation. The table does not define these considerations, but instead aims to help cybersecurity and privacy risk managers understand how IoT devices may or may not fit into their existing mitigations and/or impact how cybersecurity and privacy outcomes for their organization are currently achieved.

Challenges for Individual IoT Devices, and Risk Considerations Causing the Challenges	Affected Draft NIST SP 800-53 Revision 5 Controls	Implications for the Organization	Affected Cybersecurity Framework Subcategories
Asset Management			
Expectation 1: The device has a built-in unique identifier.			
1. The IoT device may not have a unique identifier that the organization's asset management system can access or understand. Risk Consideration 2	• CM-8, System Component Inventory	• May complicate device management, including remote access and vulnerability management.	• ID.AM-1: Physical devices and systems within the organization are inventoried
Expectation 2: The device can interface with enterprise asset management systems.			
2. The IoT device may not be able to participate in a centralized asset management system. Risk Consideration 2	• CM-8, System Component Inventory	• May have to use multiple asset management systems. • May have to perform asset management tasks manually.	• ID.AM-1: Physical devices and systems within the organization are inventoried • ID.AM-2: Software platforms and applications within the organization are inventoried • PR.DS-3: Assets are formally managed throughout removal, transfers, and disposition

Challenges for Individual IoT Devices, and Risk Considerations Causing the Challenges	Affected Draft NIST SP 800-53 Revision 5 Controls	Implications for the Organization	Affected Cybersecurity Framework Subcategories
3. The IoT device may not be directly connected to any of the organization's networks. Risk Consideration 2	• CM-8, System Component Inventory	• May have to use a separate asset management system or service, or manual asset management processes, for external IoT devices.	• ID.AM-1: Physical devices and systems within the organization are inventoried • ID.AM-2: Software platforms and applications within the organization are inventoried • PR.DS-3: Assets are formally managed throughout removal, transfers, and disposition
Expectation 3: The device can provide the organization sufficient visibility into its characteristics.			
4. The IoT device may be a black box that provides little or no information on its hardware, software, and firmware. Risk Consideration 2	• CM-8, System Component Inventory	• May complicate all aspects of device management and risk management.	• ID.AM-1: Physical devices and systems within the organization are inventoried • ID.AM-2: Software platforms and applications within the organization are inventoried • ID.AM-4: External information systems are catalogued
Expectation 4: The device or the device's manufacturer can inform the organization of all external software and services the device uses, such as software running on or dynamically downloaded from the cloud.			
5. Not all of the IoT device's external dependencies may be revealed. Risk Consideration 2	• AC-20, Use of External Systems	• Cannot manage risk for the external software and services.	• DE.CM-8: Vulnerability scans are performed • PR.IP-1: A baseline configuration of information technology/industrial control systems is created and maintained incorporating security principles (e.g. concept of least functionality) • PR.PT-3: The principle of least functionality is incorporated by configuring systems to provide only essential capabilities
Vulnerability Management			
Expectation 5: The manufacturer will provide patches or upgrades for all software and firmware throughout each device's lifespan.			
6. The manufacturer may not release patches or upgrades for the IoT device. Risk Consideration 3	• SI-2, Flaw Remediation	• Cannot remove known vulnerabilities.	• PR.IP-1: A baseline configuration of information technology/industrial control systems is created and maintained incorporating security principles (e.g. concept of least functionality)

Challenges for Individual IoT Devices, and Risk Considerations Causing the Challenges	Affected Draft NIST SP 800-53 Revision 5 Controls	Implications for the Organization	Affected Cybersecurity Framework Subcategories
7. The manufacturer may stop releasing patches and upgrades for the IoT device while it is still in use. Risk Consideration 3	• SI-2, Flaw Remediation	• May not be able to remove known vulnerabilities in the future.	• PR.IP-1: A baseline configuration of information technology/industrial control systems is created and maintained incorporating security principles (e.g. concept of least functionality)
Expectation 6: The device either has its own secure built-in patch, upgrade, and configuration management capabilities, or can interface with enterprise vulnerability management systems with such capabilities.			
8. The IoT device may not be capable of having its software patched or upgraded. Risk Considerations 2 and 3	• SI-2, Flaw Remediation	• Cannot remove known vulnerabilities.	• PR.IP-1: A baseline configuration of information technology/industrial control systems is created and maintained incorporating security principles (e.g. concept of least functionality)
9. It may be too risky to install patches or upgrades or to make configuration changes without extensive testing and preparation first, and implementing changes may require operational outages or inadvertently cause outages. Risk Consideration 1	• CM-3, Configuration Change Control • CM-6, Configuration Settings • SI-2, Flaw Remediation	• May be significant delays in removing known vulnerabilities.	• PR.IP-1: A baseline configuration of information technology/industrial control systems is created and maintained incorporating security principles (e.g. concept of least functionality)
10. The IoT device may not be able to participate in a centralized vulnerability management system. Risk Consideration 2	• CM-3, Configuration Change Control • SI-2, Flaw Remediation	• May have to use numerous vulnerability management systems instead of one. • May have to perform vulnerability management tasks manually and periodically (e.g., manually install patches, manually check for software configuration errors).	• PR.IP-1: A baseline configuration of information technology/industrial control systems is created and maintained incorporating security principles (e.g. concept of least functionality)

Challenges for Individual IoT Devices, and Risk Considerations Causing the Challenges	Affected Draft NIST SP 800-53 Revision 5 Controls	Implications for the Organization	Affected Cybersecurity Framework Subcategories
11. The IoT device may not offer the ability to change the software configuration or may not offer the features organizations want. Risk Consideration 2	• CM-2, Baseline Configuration • CM-3, Configuration Change Control • CM-6, Configuration Settings • CM-7, Least Functionality • SC-42, Sensor Capability and Data	• Cannot remove known vulnerabilities. • Cannot achieve the principle of least functionality by disabling unneeded services, functions. • Cannot restrict sensor activation and usage.	• PR.IP-1: A baseline configuration of information technology/industrial control systems is created and maintained incorporating security principles (e.g. concept of least functionality) • PR.IP-3: Configuration change control processes are in place • PR.PT-3: The principle of least functionality is incorporated by configuring systems to provide only essential capabilities
Expectation 7: The device either supports the use of vulnerability scanners or provides built-in vulnerability identification and reporting capabilities.			
12. There may not be a vulnerability scanner that can run on or against the IoT device. Risk Consideration 3	• RA-5, Vulnerability Scanning	• Cannot automatically identify known vulnerabilities.	• DE.CM-8: Vulnerability scans are performed
13. The IoT device may not offer any built-in capabilities to identify and report on known vulnerabilities. Risk Consideration 3	• RA-5, Vulnerability Scanning	• Cannot automatically identify known vulnerabilities.	• DE.CM-8: Vulnerability scans are performed
**Access Management**			
Expectation 8: The device can uniquely identify each user, device, and process attempting to logically access it.			
14. The IoT device may not support any use of identifiers. Risk Considerations 2 and 3	• IA-2, Identification and Authentication (Organizational Users) • IA-3, Device Identification and Authentication • IA-4, Identifier Management • IA-8, Identification and Authentication (Non-Organizational Users) • IA-9, Service Identification and Authentication	• Cannot identify or authenticate users, devices, and processes.	• PR.AC-1: Identities and credentials are issued, managed, verified, revoked, and audited for authorized devices, users and processes • PR.AC-7: Users, devices, and other assets are authenticated (e.g., single-factor, multi-factor) commensurate with the risk of the transaction (e.g., individuals' security and privacy risks and other organizational risks)

Challenges for Individual IoT Devices, and Risk Considerations Causing the Challenges	Affected Draft NIST SP 800-53 Revision 5 Controls	Implications for the Organization	Affected Cybersecurity Framework Subcategories
15. The IoT device may only support the use of one or more shared identifiers. Risk Considerations 2 and 3	• IA-2, Identification and Authentication (Organizational Users) • IA-3, Device Identification and Authentication • IA-4, Identifier Management • IA-8, Identification and Authentication (Non-Organizational Users) • IA-9, Service Identification and Authentication	• Cannot uniquely identify users, devices, and processes. Complicates credential management because of shared credentials.	• PR.AC-1: Identities and credentials are issued, managed, verified, revoked, and audited for authorized devices, users and processes
16. The IoT device may require the use of identifiers but only in certain cases (for example, for remote access but not local access, or for administration purposes but not regular usage). Risk Considerations 2 and 3	• IA-2, Identification and Authentication (Organizational Users) • IA-3, Device Identification and Authentication • IA-4, Identifier Management • IA-8, Identification and Authentication (Non-Organizational Users) • IA-9, Service Identification and Authentication	• Cannot identify or authenticate some users, devices, and processes.	• PR.AC-1: Identities and credentials are issued, managed, verified, revoked, and audited for authorized devices, users and processes • PR.AC-7: Users, devices, and other assets are authenticated (e.g., single-factor, multi-factor) commensurate with the risk of the transaction (e.g., individuals' security and privacy risks and other organizational risks)
Expectation 9: The device can conceal password characters from display when a person enters a password for a device, such as on a keyboard or touch screen.			
17. The IoT device may not support concealment of displayed password characters. Risk Considerations 2 and 3	• IA-6, Authenticator Feedback	• Increases the likelihood of credential theft.	• PR.AC-7: Users, devices, and other assets are authenticated (e.g., single-factor, multi-factor) commensurate with the risk of the transaction (e.g., individuals' security and privacy risks and other organizational risks)
Expectation 10: The device can authenticate each user, device, and process attempting to logically access it.			
18. The IoT device may not support use of non-trivial credentials (e.g., does not support the use of identifiers, does not allow default passwords to be changed). Risk Considerations 2 and 3	• IA-5, Authenticator Management	• Cannot identify or authenticate users, devices, and processes, which increases the chances of unauthorized access and tampering.	• PR.AC-7: Users, devices, and other assets are authenticated (e.g., single-factor, multi-factor) commensurate with the risk of the transaction (e.g., individuals' security and privacy risks and other organizational risks)

Challenges for Individual IoT Devices, and Risk Considerations Causing the Challenges	Affected Draft NIST SP 800-53 Revision 5 Controls	Implications for the Organization	Affected Cybersecurity Framework Subcategories
19. The IoT device may not support the use of strong credentials, such as cryptographic tokens or multifactor authentication, for the situations that merit them. Risk Consideration 3	• IA-5, Authenticator Management	• Increases the chances of unauthorized access and tampering through credential misuse.	• PR.AC-7: Users, devices, and other assets are authenticated (e.g., single-factor, multi-factor) commensurate with the risk of the transaction (e.g., individuals' security and privacy risks and other organizational risks)
Expectation 11: The device can use existing enterprise authenticators and authentication mechanisms.			
20. The IoT device may not support the use of an existing enterprise user authentication system. Risk Consideration 3	• IA-2, Identification and Authentication (Organizational Users) • IA-5, Authenticator Management • IA-8, Identification and Authentication (Non-Organizational Users)	• Need one or more additional accounts and credentials for each user.	• PR.AC-1: Identities and credentials are issued, managed, verified, revoked, and audited for authorized devices, users and processes • PR.AC-7: Users, devices, and other assets are authenticated (e.g., single-factor, multi-factor) commensurate with the risk of the transaction (e.g., individuals' security and privacy risks and other organizational risks)
Expectation 12: The device can restrict each user, device, and process to the minimum logical access privileges necessary.			
21. The IoT device may not support use of logical access privileges within the device that is sufficient for a given situation. Risk Consideration 3	• AC-3, Access Enforcement • AC-5, Separation of Duties • AC-6, Least Privilege	• Allows authorized users, devices, and processes to intentionally or inadvertently use privileges they should not have. • Allows an attacker who gains unauthorized access to an account to have even greater access than the account should have.	• PR.AC-4: Access permissions and authorizations are managed, incorporating the principles of least privilege and separation of duties • PR.DS-5: Protections against data leaks are implemented • PR.MA-1: Maintenance and repair of organizational assets are performed and logged, with approved and controlled tools

Challenges for Individual IoT Devices, and Risk Considerations Causing the Challenges	Affected Draft NIST SP 800-53 Revision 5 Controls	Implications for the Organization	Affected Cybersecurity Framework Subcategories
22. The IoT device may not support use of logical access privileges to restrict network communications into and out of the device that is sufficient for a given situation. Risk Consideration 3	• AC-3, Access Enforcement • AC-4, Information Flow Enforcement • AC-5, Separation of Duties • AC-6, Least Privilege • AC-17, Remote Access • SC-7, Boundary Protection	• Allows authorized users, devices, and processes to intentionally or inadvertently conduct network communications they should not be able to. • Allows an attacker to have greater network access than intended.	• PR.AC-3: Remote access is managed • PR.AC-5: Network integrity is protected (e.g., network segregation, network segmentation) • PR.DS-5: Protections against data leaks are implemented • PR.MA-2: Remote maintenance of organizational assets is approved, logged, and performed in a manner that prevents unauthorized access
Expectation 13: The device can thwart attempts to gain unauthorized access, and this feature can be configured or disabled to avoid undesired disruptions to availability. (Examples include locking or disabling an account when there are too many consecutive failed authentication attempts, delaying additional authentication attempts after failed attempts, and locking or terminating idle sessions.)			
23. The IoT device's use of these security features may not be sufficiently modifiable. Risk Considerations 1 and 3	• AC-7, Unsuccessful Logon Attempts • AC-11, Device Lock • AC-12, Session Termination • IA-11, Re-Authentication	• Cannot gain immediate access to IoT devices when needed to use or manage them.	• PR.AC-3: Remote access is managed • PR.AC-4: Access permissions and authorizations are managed, incorporating the principles of least privilege and separation of duties • PR.MA-1: Maintenance and repair of organizational assets are performed and logged, with approved and controlled tools • PR.MA-2: Remote maintenance of organizational assets is approved, logged, and performed in a manner that prevents unauthorized access

Challenges for Individual IoT Devices, and Risk Considerations Causing the Challenges	Affected Draft NIST SP 800-53 Revision 5 Controls	Implications for the Organization	Affected Cybersecurity Framework Subcategories
Expectation 14: The device has adequate built-in physical security controls to protect it from tampering (e.g., tamper-resistant packaging).			
24. The IoT device may be deployed in an area where people who are not authorized to access the device may do so or where authorized people can access the device in unauthorized ways. Risk Considerations 1 and 2	• MP-2, Media Access • MP-7, Media Use • PE-3, Physical Access Control	• Allows an attacker to have direct physical access to devices and tamper with them, including adding or removing storage media, connecting peripherals, etc.	• PR.AC-2: Physical access to assets is managed and protected • PR.PT-2: Removable media is protected and its use restricted according to policy • PR.MA-1: Maintenance and repair of organizational assets are performed and logged, with approved and controlled tools
Incident Detection			
Expectation 15: The device can log its operational and security events.			
25. The IoT device may not be able to log its operational and security events at all or in sufficient detail. Risk Consideration 3	• AU-2, Audit Events • AU-3, Content of Audit Records • AU-12, Audit Generation • SI-4, System Monitoring	• Increases the likelihood of malicious activity going undetected. • Cannot confirm and reconstruct incidents from log entries.	• DE.CM-7: Monitoring for unauthorized personnel, connections, devices, and software is performed • PR.PT-1: Audit/log records are determined, documented, implemented, and reviewed in accordance with policy • RS.AN-1: Notifications from detection systems are investigated
26. The IoT device may continue operating even when a logging failure occurs. Risk Consideration 3	• AU-5, Response to Audit Processing Failures	• Increased likelihood of malicious activity going undetected.	• DE.CM-7: Monitoring for unauthorized personnel, connections, devices, and software is performed • PR.PT-1: Audit/log records are determined, documented, implemented, and reviewed in accordance with policy
Expectation 16: The device can interface with existing enterprise log management systems.			
27. The IoT device may not be able to participate in an enterprise log management system. Risk Consideration 2	• AU-6, Audit Review, Analysis, and Reporting • SI-4, System Monitoring	• May have to use numerous log management systems instead of one. • May have to perform log management tasks manually. • Increases the likelihood of malicious activity going undetected.	• DE.AE-3: Event data are collected and correlated from multiple sources and sensors • DE.CM-7: Monitoring for unauthorized personnel, connections, devices, and software is performed • PR.PT-1: Audit/log records are determined, documented, implemented, and reviewed in accordance with policy

Challenges for Individual IoT Devices, and Risk Considerations Causing the Challenges	Affected Draft NIST SP 800-53 Revision 5 Controls	Implications for the Organization	Affected Cybersecurity Framework Subcategories
Expectation 17: The device can facilitate the detection of potential incidents by internal or external controls, such as intrusion prevention systems, anti-malware utilities, and file integrity checking mechanisms.			
28. The IoT device may not be able to execute internal detection controls or interact with external detection controls without adversely affecting device operation. Risk Considerations 1 and 3	• SI-3, Malicious Code Protection • SI-7, Software, Firmware, and Information Integrity	• Increases the likelihood of malicious code infections and other unauthorized activities occurring and going undetected.	• DE.CM-1: The network is monitored to detect potential cybersecurity events • DE.CM-4: Malicious code is detected • PR.DS-6: Integrity checking mechanisms are used to verify software, firmware, and information integrity
29. The IoT device may not provide controls with the visibility needed to detect incidents efficiently and effectively. Risk Considerations 2 and 3	• IR-4, Incident Handling • SI-4, System Monitoring	• Increases the likelihood of malicious code and other unauthorized activities going undetected.	• DE.CM-1: The network is monitored to detect potential cybersecurity events • DE.CM-4: Malicious code is detected • PR.DS-6: Integrity checking mechanisms are used to verify software, firmware, and information integrity
Expectation 18: The device can support event and incident analysis activities.			
30. The IoT device may not provide analysts with sufficient access to the device's resources in order to do the necessary analysis. Risk Considerations 2 and 3	• SI-4, System Monitoring	• Cannot use forensic tools for information gathering and analysis.	• RS.AN-1: Notifications from detection systems are investigated • RS.AN-3: Forensics are performed

4.2 Potential Challenges with Achieving Goal 2, Protect Data Security

Table 2 follows the same conventions as Table 1, but for protecting data security. It is assumed that if data security needs to be protected, device security needs protection as well, so the challenges in both tables would need to be considered.

Note that the Incident Detection section of Table 1 is also applicable for protecting data security. Table 1 assumes only device security incidents need to be protected; the same potential challenges, affected controls, implications, and Cybersecurity Framework subcategories also apply to detecting data security incidents. The Incident Detection rows are omitted from Table 2 for brevity.

Table 2: Potential Challenges with Achieving Goal 2, Protect Data Security

Challenges for Individual IoT Devices	Affected Draft NIST SP 800-53 Revision 5 Controls	Implications for the Organization	Affected Cybersecurity Framework Subcategories
Data Protection			
Expectation 19: The device can prevent unauthorized access to all sensitive data on its storage devices.			
31. The IoT device may not provide sufficiently strong encryption capabilities for its stored data. Risk Consideration 3	• MP-4, Media Storage • SC-28, Protection of Information at Rest	• Increases the likelihood of unauthorized access to or tampering with sensitive data.	• PR.DS-1: Data-at-rest is protected • PR.PT-2: Removable media is protected and its use restricted according to policy
32. The IoT device may not provide a mechanism for sanitizing sensitive data before disposing of or repurposing the device. Risk Consideration 3	• MP-6, Media Sanitization	• Increases the likelihood of unauthorized access to sensitive data.	• PR.IP-6: Data is destroyed according to policy
Expectation 20: The device has a mechanism to support data availability through secure backups.			
33. The IoT device may not provide a secure backup and restore mechanism for its data. Risk Consideration 3	• CP-9, System Backup	• Increases the likelihood of loss of data.	• PR.IP-4: Backups of information are conducted, maintained, and tested
Expectation 21: The device can prevent unauthorized access to all sensitive data transmitted from it over networks.			
34. The IoT device may not provide sufficiently strong encryption capabilities for protecting sensitive data sent in its network communications. Risk Consideration 3	• AC-18, Wireless Access • SC-8, Transmission Confidentiality and Integrity	• Increases the likelihood of eavesdropping on communications.	• PR.DS-2: Data-in-transit is protected
35. The IoT device may not verify the identity of another computing device before sending sensitive data in its network communications. Risk Consideration 3	• SC-8, Transmission Confidentiality and Integrity • SC-23, Session Authenticity	• Increases the likelihood of eavesdropping, interception, manipulation, impersonation, and other forms of attack on communications.	• PR.DS-2: Data-in-transit is protected

4.3 Potential Challenges with Achieving Goal 3, Protect Individuals' Privacy

Table 3 lists potential challenges with achieving goal 3, protecting individuals' privacy by mitigating privacy risk arising from authorized PII processing. It follows the same conventions as the previous tables, but it omits mappings to Cybersecurity Framework Subcategories since the Cybersecurity Framework does not address privacy risks from authorized PII processing. It is assumed that if individuals' privacy needs to be protected, device and data security need to be protected as well, so the challenges in all three tables would need to be considered. However, organizations may use information from Table 2 to address privacy risks arising from the loss of confidentiality, integrity, or availability of PII.

Table 3: Potential Challenges with Achieving Goal 3, Protect Individuals' Privacy

Challenges for Individual IoT Devices	Affected Draft NIST SP 800-53 Revision 5 Controls	Implications for the Organization
Disassociated Data Management		
Expectation 22: The device operates in a traditional federated identity environment.		
36. The IoT device may contribute data that is used for identification and authentication, but is outside of traditional federated environments. Risk Consideration 3	IA-8 (6), Identification and Authentication (non-organizational users) | Disassociability	• Techniques such as the use of identifier mapping tables and privacy-enhancing cryptographic techniques to blind credential service providers and relying parties from each other or to make identity attributes less visible to transmitting parties may not work outside a traditional federated environment.
Informed Decision Making		
Expectation 23: Traditional interfaces exist for individual engagement with the device.		
37. The IoT device may lack interfaces that enable individuals to interact with it. Risk Consideration 2	IP-2, Consent	• Individuals may not be able to provide consent for the processing of their PII or condition further processing of specific attributes.
38. Decentralized data processing functions and heterogenous ownership of IoT devices challenge traditional accountability processes. Risk Consideration 3	IP-3, Redress	• Individuals may not be able to locate the source of inaccurate or otherwise problematic PII in order to correct it or fix the problem.
39. The IoT device may lack interfaces that enable individuals to read privacy notices. Risk Consideration 2	IP-4, Privacy Notice	• Individuals may not be able to read or access privacy notices.
40. The IoT device may lack interfaces to enable access to PII, or PII may be stored in unknown locations. Risk Consideration 2	IP-6, Individual Access	• Individuals may have difficulty accessing their information, which curtails their ability to manage their information and understand what is happening with their data, and increases compliance risks.
PII Processing Permissions Management		
Expectation 24: There is sufficient centralized control to apply policy or regulatory requirements to PII.		
41. The IoT device may collect PII indiscriminately or analyze, share, or act upon the PII based on automated processes. Risk Consideration 2	PA-2, Authority to Collect	• PII may be processed in ways that are out of compliance with regulatory requirements or an organization's policies.
42. IoT devices may be complex and dynamic, with sensing functionality that can collect PII being frequently added and removed. Risk Consideration 1	PA-3, Purpose Specification	• PII may be hard to track such that individuals, as well as device owners/operators, may not have reliable assumptions about how PII is being processed, causing informed decision making to be more difficult.

Challenges for Individual IoT Devices	Affected Draft NIST SP 800-53 Revision 5 Controls	Implications for the Organization
43. The IoT device may be accessed remotely, allowing the sharing of PII outside the control of the administrator. Risk Consideration 2	PA-4, Information Sharing with External Parties	• PII may be shared in ways that are out of compliance with regulatory requirements or an organization's policies.
Information Flow Management		
Expectation 25: There is sufficient centralized control to manage PII.		
44. IoT devices may be complex and dynamic, with sensing functionality that can collect PII being frequently added and removed. Risk Consideration 1	PM-29, Inventory of Personally Identifiable Information	• PII may be difficult to identify and track using traditional inventory methods.
45. IoT devices may not support standardized mechanisms for centralized data management, and the sheer number of IoT devices to manage may be overwhelming. Risk Consideration 2	SC-7 (24), Boundary Protection | Personally Identifiable Information	• Application of PII processing rules intended to protect individuals' privacy may be disrupted.
46. The IoT device may not have the capability to support configurations such as remote activation prevention, limited data reporting, notice of collection, and data minimization. Risk Consideration 3	SC-42, Sensor Capability and Data	• Lack of direct privacy risk mitigation capabilities may require compensating controls and may impact an organization's ability to optimize the amount of privacy risk that can be reduced.
47. The IoT device may indiscriminately collect PII. Heterogenous ownership of devices challenges traditional data management techniques. Risk Consideration 2	SI-12 (1), Information Management and Retention | Limit Personally Identifiable Information Elements	• It is more likely that operationally unnecessary PII will be retained.
48. Decentralized data processing functions and heterogenous ownership of IoT devices challenge traditional data management processes with respect to checking for accuracy of data. Risk Consideration 2	SI-19, Data Quality Operations	• It is more likely that inaccurate PII will persist, with the potential to create problems for individuals.
49. Decentralized data processing functions and heterogenous ownership of IoT devices challenge traditional de-identification processes. Risk Considerations 2 and 3	SI-20, De-Identification	• Aggregation of disparate data sets may lead to re-identification of PII.

5   Recommendations for Addressing Cybersecurity and Privacy Risk Mitigation Challenges for IoT Devices

This section provides recommendations for addressing the cybersecurity and privacy risk mitigation challenges for IoT devices. Figure 6 summarizes the recommendations, which are listed below and, if indicated, described in more detail elsewhere in the publication:

Figure 6: Recommendation Summary

1. Understand the IoT device risk considerations (Section 3) and the challenges they may cause to mitigating cybersecurity and privacy risks for IoT devices in the appropriate risk mitigation areas (Section 4).

2. Adjust organizational policies and processes to address the cybersecurity and privacy risk mitigation challenges throughout the IoT device lifecycle. Section 5.1 provides more information on this. Section 4 of this publication cites many examples of possible challenges, but each organization will need to customize these to take into account mission requirements and other organization-specific characteristics.

3. Implement updated mitigation practices for the organization's IoT devices as you would any other changes to practices (Section 5.2).

5.1   Adjusting Organizational Policies and Processes

Organizations should ensure they are addressing the considerations throughout the IoT device lifecycle in their cybersecurity and privacy policies and processes. Organizations should ensure they clearly state how they scope IoT in order to avoid confusion and ambiguity. This is particularly important for organizations that may be subject to laws and regulations with differing definitions of IoT.

Similarly, organizations should ensure their cybersecurity, supply chain, and privacy risk management programs take IoT into account appropriately. This includes the following:

*   Determining which devices have IoT device capabilities. Have mechanisms in place to determine whether a device that might be procured or has already been procured is an IoT device, if that is not apparent.

*   Identifying IoT device types. Know which types of IoT devices are in use, which capabilities each type supports, and what purposes each type supports.

- Assessing IoT device risk. It is important to take into consideration the particular IoT environment the IoT devices reside within, and not just assess risks for IoT devices in isolation. For example, attaching an actuator to one physical system may affect risks much differently than attaching the same actuator to another physical system.

- Determining how to respond to that risk by accepting, avoiding, mitigating, sharing, or transferring it. As previously discussed, some risk mitigation strategies for conventional IT may not work well for IoT. Section 4 of this publication discusses risk mitigation challenges for IoT devices in considerable detail.

Managing cybersecurity and privacy risks for some IoT devices may affect other types of risks and introduce new risks to safety, reliability, resiliency, performance, and other areas. Organizations should be sure to consider the tradeoffs among these risks when making decisions about cybersecurity and privacy risk mitigation. For example, suppose a particular IoT device is critical for safety. Requiring personnel in a physically secured area to enter a password in order to gain local access to the IoT device could delay intervention during a malfunction. Additional requirements involving password length, password complexity, and automatic account lockouts after consecutive failed authentication attempts could cause far longer delays, increasing the likelihood and magnitude of harm. Organizations should leverage their existing programs for managing other forms of risk when determining how IoT device cybersecurity and privacy risks should be managed.

Based on the potential mitigation challenges and the implications of those challenges, the implementations of the following Cybersecurity Framework Subcategories [6] are most likely to need adjustments so the organizational policies and processes adequately address cybersecurity risk throughout the IoT device lifecycle:

- ID.AM (Identify—Asset Management)

  o ID.AM-1: Physical devices and systems within the organization are inventoried
  o ID.AM-2: Software platforms and applications within the organization are inventoried

- ID.BE (Identify—Business Environment)

  o ID.BE-4: Dependencies and critical functions for delivery of critical services are established
  o ID.BE-5: Resilience requirements to support delivery of critical services are established for all operating states (e.g. under duress/attack, during recovery, normal operations)

- ID.GV (Identify—Governance)

  o ID.GV-1: Organizational cybersecurity policy is established and communicated
  o ID.GV-2: Cybersecurity roles and responsibilities are coordinated and aligned with internal roles and external partners
  o ID.GV-3: Legal and regulatory requirements regarding cybersecurity, including privacy and civil liberties obligations, are understood and managed
  o ID.GV-4: Governance and risk management processes address cybersecurity risks

- ID.RA (Identify—Risk Assessment)

  o ID.RA-1: Asset vulnerabilities are identified and documented
  o ID.RA-3: Threats, both internal and external, are identified and documented
  o ID.RA-4: Potential business impacts and likelihoods are identified
  o ID.RA-6: Risk responses are identified and prioritized

- ID.RM (Identify—Risk Management Strategy)

  o ID.RM-2: Organizational risk tolerance is determined and clearly expressed
  o ID.RM-3: The organization's determination of risk tolerance is informed by its role in critical infrastructure and sector specific risk analysis

- ID.SC (Identify—Supply Chain Risk Management)

  o ID.SC-2: Suppliers and third party partners of information systems, components, and services are identified, prioritized, and assessed using a cyber supply chain risk assessment process
  o ID.SC-3: Contracts with suppliers and third-party partners are used to implement appropriate measures designed to meet the objectives of an organization's cybersecurity program and Cyber Supply Chain Risk Management Plan

- PR.IP (Protect—Information Protection Processes and Procedures)

  o PR.IP-3: Configuration change control processes are in place
  o PR.IP-9: Response plans (Incident Response and Business Continuity) and recovery plans (Incident Recovery and Disaster Recovery) are in place and managed
  o PR.IP-12: A vulnerability management plan is developed and implemented

Similarly, the implementations of the tasks listed below from NIST SP 800-37 Revision 2 [4] are most likely to need adjusted so the organizational policies and processes adequately address cybersecurity and privacy risk throughout the IoT device lifecycle. Note that although the Cybersecurity Framework can be used to manage the aspect of privacy relating to PII cybersecurity, NIST SP 800-37 Revision 2 can be used to manage the full scope of privacy because it integrates authorized PII processing into the NIST Risk Management Framework (RMF).

- Prepare, Organization Level, Task P-1: Risk Management Roles

- Prepare, Organization Level, Task P-2: Risk Management Strategy

- Prepare, Organization Level, Task P-3: Risk Assessment—Organization

- Prepare, System Level, Task P-8: Mission or Business Focus

- Prepare, System Level, Task P-13: Information Life Cycle

- Prepare, System Level, Task P-14: Risk Assessment—System

- Prepare, System Level, Task P-15: Requirements Definition

5.2   Implementing Updated Risk Mitigation Practices

An organization's cybersecurity and privacy risk mitigation practices may need significant changes because of the sheer number of IoT devices and the large number of IoT device types. For conventional IT devices, most organizations have dozens of types—desktops, laptops, servers, smartphones, routers, switches, firewalls, printers, etc. Conventional IT devices within a single type tend to have similar capabilities. For example, most laptops have similar data storage and processing capabilities; human user interface and network interface capabilities; and supporting capabilities, such as centralized management. This enables organizations to determine how to manage risk for each of the dozens of conventional IT device types, with some customizations for particular devices and device models, and organizations are generally accustomed to this level of effort.

In contrast, most organizations may have many more types of IoT devices than conventional IT devices because of the single-purpose nature of most IoT devices. An organization may need to determine how to manage risk for hundreds or thousands of IoT device types. Capabilities vary widely from one IoT device type to another, with one type lacking data storage and centralized management capabilities, and another type having numerous sensors and actuators, using local and remote data storage and processing capabilities, and being connected to several internal and external networks at once. The variability in capabilities causes similar variability in the cybersecurity and privacy risks involving each IoT device type, as well as the options for mitigating those risks.

In addition, an organization may need to determine how to manage risk not just by device type, but also by device usage. The way a device is to be used may indicate that one security objective, such as integrity, is more important than another, such as confidentiality, and that in turn may necessitate different mechanisms to risk mitigation. Similarly, a device might be used in such a way that some of its capabilities are not needed and can be disabled, which could reduce the device's risk.

Appendix A—[Withdrawn]

Appendix A previously held examples of possible cybersecurity and privacy capabilities that organizations may want their IoT devices to have. That content has been removed from this publication and will be refined and released in a separate publication which will be posted to our program website (https://www.nist.gov/programs-projects/nist-cybersecurity-iot-program).

Appendix B—Acronyms and Abbreviations

Selected acronyms and abbreviations used in this paper are defined below.

API

IoT   Internet of Things
IP   Internet Protocol
IR   Internal Report
IT   Information Technology
ITL   Information Technology Laboratory
LTE

OT   Operational Technology
PII   Personally Identifiable Information
RFC

SLA   Service Level Agreement
SP   Special Publication

Appendix C—Glossary

Actuating Capability	The ability to change something in the physical world.
Application Interface Capability	The ability for other computing devices to communicate with an IoT device through an IoT device application.
Capability	A feature or function.
Data Actions	"System operations that process PII." [5]
Disassociability	"Enabling the processing of PII or events without association to individuals or devices beyond the operational requirements of the system." [5]
Human User Interface Capability	The ability for an IoT device to communicate directly with people.
Interface Capabilities	Capabilities which enable interactions involving IoT devices (e.g., device-to-device communications, human-to-device communications). The types of interface capabilities are application, human user, and network.
Network Interface Capability	The ability to interface with a communication network for the purpose of communicating data to or from an IoT device. A network interface capability allows a device to be connected to and use a communication network. Every IoT device has at least one network interface capability and may have more than one.
Personally Identifiable Information (PII)	"Information that can be used to distinguish or trace an individual's identity, either alone or when combined with other information that is linked or linkable to a specific individual." [8]
PII Processing	
	A cybersecurity or privacy capability built into an IoT device. Pre-market capabilities are integrated into IoT devices by the manufacturer or vendor before they are shipped to customer organizations.
Problematic Data Action	A system operation that processes PII through the information lifecycle and as a side effect causes individuals to experience some type of problem(s).

Risk	"A measure of the extent to which an entity is threatened by a potential circumstance or event, and typically is a function of: (i) the adverse impact, or magnitude of harm, that would arise if the circumstance or event occurs; and (ii) the likelihood of occurrence." [4]
Sensing Capability	The ability to provide an observation of an aspect of the physical world in the form of measurement data.
Supporting Capabilities	Capabilities that provide functionality that supports the other IoT capabilities. Examples of supporting capabilities are device management, cybersecurity, and privacy capabilities.
Transducer Capabilities	Capabilities that provide the ability for computing devices to interact directly with physical entities of interest. The two types of transducer capabilities are sensing and actuating.

Appendix D—References

[1]   Newhouse W, Keith S, Scribner B, Witte G (2017) National Initiative for Cybersecurity
        Education (NICE) Cybersecurity Workforce Framework. (National Institute of
        Standards and Technology, Gaithersburg, MD), NIST Special Publication (SP) 800-181.
        https://doi.org/10.6028/NIST.SP.800-181

[2]   Simmon E (forthcoming) A Model for the Internet of Things (IoT). (National Institute
        of Standards and Technology, Gaithersburg, MD).

[3]   Stouffer K, Pillitteri V, Lightman S, Abrams M, Hahn A (2015) Guide to Industrial
        Control Systems (ICS) Security. (National Institute of Standards and Technology,
        Gaithersburg, MD), NIST Special Publication (SP) 800-82, Rev. 2.
        https://doi.org/10.6028/NIST.SP.800-82r2

[4]   Joint Task Force (2018) Risk Management Framework for Information Systems and
        Organizations: A System Life Cycle Approach for Security and Privacy. (National
        Institute of Standards and Technology, Gaithersburg, MD), NIST Special Publication
        (SP) 800-37, Rev. 2. https://doi.org/10.6028/NIST.SP.800-37r2

[5]   Brooks S, Garcia M, Lefkovitz N, Lightman S, Nadeau E (2017) An Introduction to
        Privacy Engineering and Risk Management in Federal Systems. (National Institute of
        Standards and Technology, Gaithersburg, MD), NIST Interagency or Internal Report
        (IR) 8062. https://doi.org/10.6028/NIST.IR.8062

[6]   National Institute of Standards and Technology (2018) Framework for Improving
        Critical Infrastructure Cybersecurity, Version 1.1. (National Institute of Standards and
        Technology, Gaithersburg, MD). https://doi.org/10.6028/NIST.CSWP.04162018

[7]   Joint Task Force (2017) Security and Privacy Controls for Information Systems and
        Organizations. (National Institute of Standards and Technology, Gaithersburg, MD),
        Draft NIST Special Publication (SP) 800-53, Rev. 5.
        https://csrc.nist.gov/publications/detail/sp/800-53/rev-5/draft

[8]   Office of Management and Budget (2016) Managing Information as a Strategic
        Resource. (Office of Management and Budget (OMB), Washington, DC), OMB
        Circular No. A-130.
        https://www.whitehouse.gov/sites/whitehouse.gov/files/omb/circulars/A130/a130revise
        d.pdf